Of Course!

The Greatest Collection Of Riddles &
Brain Teasers For Expanding Your Mind

Zack Guido

Dedicated to the open-minded, the gifted, and the forward-moving.

TABLE OF CONTENTS

INTRODUCTION

What you are about to read is a curated collection of riddles and brain teasers that has been compiled and refined over many years. They present challenging scenarios that stimulate your brain and engage the problem-solving portion of your mind.

The riddles vary in style, difficulty, and complexity. Situations involving high-level mathematics were avoided, though a handful of math-based problems are included.

- There should be no solution that requires more than a basic high-school level of competency.

- There are no riddles that rely on wordplay or linguistic devices.

- There are no 'trick questions'.

In this book you will figure out how to cross bridges, how to escape from prison cells, how to steal rope, how to shoot cyborgs, how to transport bananas through the desert, how to figure out the color of a hat you have on, how to turn on light bulbs, and how to save hundreds of peoples' lives.

The first three questions are meant to be a warm-up. They should help to get you into the right state of mind and ready you for the problems that follow. Enjoy.

THE RIDDLES

1. Redmond's Question
(solution on page 35)

Why are manhole covers round?

2. Eating Garbage
(solution on page 36)

You're having a conversation with a friend about your favorite foods. He says to you, "My favorite food is the one where you throw away the outside and cook the inside, then you eat the outside and throw away the inside!"

What food is he talking about?

3. Fox Trotting
(solution on page 37)

How far can a fox run into the woods?

4. Fork In The Road
(solution on page 38)

You are a stranger lost in a strange land. You are travelling along a road and come to an intersection where you can either go east or west. You know that one of these roads will lead you to your destination, and that the other will lead you to a hopeless despair. Standing at this fork in the road are two men who know the direction you must take to reach your destination. You know that one of these men always tells the truth and that the other always lies. Unfortunately, you cannot remember who is who.

With only one question directed towards one of the men, how can you be sure to make the right choice and travel down the correct path?

5. River Dilemma
(solution on page 39)

You have just purchased three things at the local market: a wolf, a duck, and a bag of seeds. To get back home you must travel across a river in a small boat. You are only allowed to have one item with you on your boat at any time. You cannot leave the wolf alone with the duck, because the wolf will eat the duck. You cannot leave the duck alone with the bag of seeds, because the duck will eat the seeds.

How many trips on the boat must you take to be able to get the wolf, duck, and bag of seeds across to the other side of the river safely?

6. Circular Divisions
(solution on page 40)

What is the maximum number of sections into which a circle may be divided into by drawing four straight lines through it?

7. French Toasting
(solution on page 41)

You are making some French toast for breakfast. In order to cook a perfect piece of French toast you must fry each side of the slice of bread for thirty seconds. You only have one frying pan and it can only hold two slices of bread at a time.

How quickly can you make three perfect slices of French toast?

8. Flipping Two Coins
(solution on page 42)

Your friend flips two coins behind your back and tells you: "At least one of the coins came up tails." What is the probability that both coins came up tails?

9. Nuts, Bolts, Nuts & Bolts
(solution on page 43)

In front of you are three closed metal boxes. One is labeled "Nuts", one is labeled "Bolts", and one is labeled "Nuts & Bolts". You know that every box is incorrectly labeled and you would like to rearrange the labels so that each box is correct.

By making only one selection from one box, how can you be sure to properly re-label each box?

10. Cake Slicing
(solution on page 44)

You have a delicious round birthday cake. How many equal-sized pieces can you cut the cake into by making only three straight slices with a knife and without moving any of the pieces?

11. Halfway Glass
(solution on page 45)

You are in an empty room with a glass of water. The glass is a right cylinder that looks like it is about half-full, but you are not quite sure. What is the most accurate way, without spilling any water, to determine whether the glass is half-full, more than half-full, or less than half-full?

12. A Hanging Chain
(solution on page 46)

A thin four-foot long chain is suspended by its ends and nailed to a wall. Both nails are level with one another and parallel to the floor. Because of gravity, the middle part of the chain hangs down towards the floor. If the vertical length of the chain is two feet, what is the distance between the two nails?

13. The Loaded Coin
(solution on page 47)

You and your best friend have loved the same girl since kindergarten. After years and years of discussions, arguments, and fights, you have both decided to settle the matter with a coin toss. The only coin available to you is an old wooden nickel and you are certain that it comes up heads more than 50% of the time. How can you be sure to have a fair contest that is based purely on chance by only flipping this coin?

14. Who Makes What?
(solution on page 48)

You and two of you friends would like to know the average of all of your salaries. You are each self-conscious about the amount of money you make and will not tell one another your salaries. What can you do to figure out the average salary?

15. Water Buckets
(solution on page 49)

You have a 5-gallon bucket, a 3-gallon bucket, and a water faucet. How can you accurately put four gallons of water into the 5-gallon bucket?

16. Prison Escape
(solution on page 50)

A man is imprisoned in a ten-foot by ten-foot by ten-foot room. The walls are made of concrete, the floor is made out of dirt, and the only openings are a locked door and a skylight. The man has a small shovel and starts to dig a hole in the floor. He knows that it is impossible to tunnel out of the prison cell, but he continues to dig anyways.

What is the man's plan?

17. <u>The Dove In The Hand</u>
(solution on page 51)

An old wise man lived in a little home on a hill. One morning, two young boys from the town decided they wanted to fool the wise man. They took a dove with them and knocked on the old man's door. When he answered, one of the boys said to him: "Lets see how smart you really are! Is the dove I'm holding behind my back dead or alive?" The old man smiled and replied, "I cannot answer you because I know you are trying to trick me."

Despite knowing the condition of the dove, why wouldn't the wise old man answer the young boy?

18. <u>Stones, Jars, Life, Death</u>
(solution on page 52)

You are a prisoner in a strange land. You have been sentenced to death but are being given one chance to live. The king of the land has decided to let you play a simple game to determine your fate:

You are presented with two clay jars, one containing 100 white stones, and one containing 100 black stones. You are allowed to redistribute these stones any way that you like, but when you are finished all stones must be in the jars. After you have finished, both jars will be shaken up, you will be blindfolded, and you will be presented one of the two jars at random. You will pick one stone out of the jar given to you. If the stone is white, your life will be spared, if the stone is black, you will be executed immediately.

How should you redistribute the stones to give yourself the best chance of survival?

19. <u>Immanuel The Clock Setter</u>
(solution on page 53)

Immanuel was on his way out the door to visit an old friend across the village when he realized that his grandfather clock had stopped and no longer displayed the correct time. This was the only clock in his home and the man owned no watches or other time-telling devices. Without disappointment Immanuel left his home and walked roughly three miles to his friend's house. He glanced at the friend's wall clock as he entered the house and after visiting for a few hours set off back home along the same route. He walked at the same pace home and had no idea of knowing how long his trip back took him. Regardless, when Immanuel got back home he immediately went to his grandfather clock and set it to the correct time.

How did he know what time it was?

20. <u>The Coin Flipping Game</u>
(solution on page 54)

Your friend has a coin and asks you if you want to play a game: "I will flip this coin until the number of heads flipped is equal to the number of tails flipped. Then I will give you a dollar for each time I flipped the coin."

What are the chances that you play this game with your friend once and he pays you exactly eight dollars?

21. <u>The Scale Of All Scales</u>
(solution on page 55)

You have in front of you a standard balance scale. What is the fewest number of weights that you would need to be able to accurately weigh any object that weighs between one and one hundred pounds (rounded up to the nearest pound)? What are the weights?

22. Something Wicked Which Way Comes?
(solution on page 56)

Jim woke up with intentions to go to the carnival that just arrived in town. He left his home and headed towards the town square, not quite sure if he was walking in the right direction. He approached the first person he saw and asked them, "Am I headed towards the carnival?" Unfortunately this person was unable to speak and simply rubbed their stomach in response. Jim knew that this meant either yes or no but was not sure which. With just one additional question, Jim was able to find out.

What did Jim ask?

23. Water Buckets II
(solution on page 57)

You have a 12-gallon bucket, an 8-gallon bucket, and a 5-gallon bucket. The 12-gallon bucket is full of water and the other two are empty. Without using any additional water how can you divide the twelve gallons of water equally so that two of the three buckets have exactly six gallons of water in them?

24. Making Change
(solution on page 58)

What is the maximum value of change that you can have in U.S. coins (pennies, nickels, dimes, and quarters) without being able to give someone exact change for a one-dollar bill?

25. Race To The Finish

(solution on page 59)

A wise old man is on his deathbed and must decide which of his two sons will inherit his large fortune. He calls both of his sons into the room and says to them, "the two of you will ride your horses around the track in a race to determine who will inherit my fortune. Whichever horse crosses the finish line last will win my entire fortune for its owner!" The two men sit puzzled for a few minutes trying to understand how to make sense of a race where the losing horse wins. After a while they both give up and ask their father for advice regarding this situation. He tells them something and as soon as he finishes his sentence the two brothers rush out to the track and race.

What did the wise old man say to his two sons?

26. Five Hats In A Box

(solution on page 60)

There is a box in front of you with three black hats and two white hats inside. Three perfectly intelligent men, Alan, Bob, and Cal, who each know the contents of the box, are blindfolded and asked to reach into the box, take a hat, and place it on their heads. They do not know which color hat they have taken and cannot see the hats on their own heads. You then place the three men in a single file line in such a way that after you remove their blindfolds Alan can see Bob and Cal's hats, Bob can see Cal's hat, and Cal cannot see anyone's hat. The men are required to face forward and are not allowed to turn around.

You ask Alan if he knows the color of the hat he is wearing and he replies, "no." You then ask Bob if he knows the color of the hat he is wearing and he too replies, "no." Finally, you ask Cal if he knows the color of the hat he is wearing and he answers, "actually I do!"

What color hat was Cal wearing and how did he figure this out?

27. Weighing Fake Coins
(solution on page 61)

There is a table in front of you with an electronic scale and ten groups of ten coins. You know that one of these groups of coins contains all counterfeit coins, but you don't know which group it is. You know that the real coins each weigh one ounce and that the counterfeit coins only weigh half an ounce.

Using just the coins and the scale, what is the fewest number of weighings you have to make to find the counterfeit coins?

28. Two Hourglasses
(solution on page 62)

There is a table in front of you with two hourglasses. One contains seven minutes of sand and the other contains eleven minutes of sand. Using just these two hourglasses, how can you accurately time fifteen minutes?

29. Last Words?
(solution on page 63)

You have committed a terrible crime and tomorrow morning you will be taken to the town square and executed. The executioner has taken a liking to you and decides to do you a favor and allow you a choice in your execution method. You are allowed to make one final statement: If this statement is true, you will be hanged in the morning. If this statement is false you will be beheaded in the morning.

What should your final statement be?

30. An Evil Mayor
(solution on page 64)

A dilemma has come up in your village between a farmer, his daughter, and the mayor. The farmer owes the mayor a sum of money that he cannot pay back and the mayor is in love with the farmer's daughter. This is upsetting to the daughter as she finds the mayor to be an evil, ugly, and cruel man. The mayor tells the farmer that he will settle the debt in front of the whole village by playing a simple game:

The mayor will take a black stone and a white stone and place them in a bag. The farmer's daughter will reach into the bag and draw one of the stones out in front of the whole village. If she draws the white stone, the farmer's debt would be forgiven and everything would return to normal. If she draws the black stone, she will be forced to marry the mayor and the debt will not be forgiven. Considering the situation, the farmer has no choice but to agree to this settlement. The daughter knows the mayor too well and believes that he will cheat and put two black stones into the bag.

What can she do to get out of marrying the mayor and have her father's debt forgiven?

31. Mixing Medicine
(solution on page 65)

You have been feeling very sick lately and decide to visit your doctor. He gives you two medications to take, Medicine Y and Medicine X. You are instructed to take one pill of each every day and the pills must be taken together. If you take less than this amount you will die from illness, and if you take more you will die from an overdose. When putting the pills away in your medicine cabinet you accidentally drop the bottles and three pills fall out. You count the remaining pills in each bottle and determine that on the floor there is one X pill and two Y pills. Unfortunately the pills look identical and you have no way of telling them apart.

How can you save the pills on the floor and still maintain the proper daily dosage and take all of the pills?

32. Three Light Bulbs & Three Switches
(solution on page 66)

You are standing in a room with three light switches. Each of these switches controls one of three light bulbs in the room next to you. All of the switches are initially down and in the off position, and you are told that all of the light bulbs in the other room are off.

If you are allowed only one chance to enter the room with the three light bulbs, how can you determine which switches go with which bulbs?

33. A Spinning Disk
(solution on page 67)

On a table in front of you is a spinning disk, much like a vinyl record on a turntable. One half of the disk's surface is colored white, and the other half is colored black. The disk is spinning so fast that you are not able to tell which direction it is spinning. You also have an unlimited number of color sensors that will light up when the surface below them is black.

How many of these sensors would you have to place and where would you place them to determine which way the disk is spinning?

34. Bridge Crossing
(solution on page 68)

Alan, Bob, Cal, and Dan are all on one side of a narrow and dangerous bridge that they would like to cross. It is late at night and very dark so they cannot cross safely without a flashlight. They have only one flashlight and the bridge is only strong enough to support the weight of two people at once. Each of the four people walk at different speeds: Alan can cross the bridge in one minute, Bob can cross in two minutes, Cal can cross in five minutes, and Dan can cross in ten minutes. When two people are walking together sharing the flashlight they walk at the slower person's pace.

How quickly can Alan, Bob, Cal, and Dan all get across the bridge safely?

35. Force Field Detainment
(solution on page 69)

You have been given the duty of guarding a group of prisoners that are trapped in a force field. The prisoners are all very brave and will attempt to escape on any positive probability of success. You have a gun with only one bullet but you have perfect accuracy and will always hit your target. One of the jail's technicians needs to make a critical adjustment to the force field generator and for one minute the force field will be shut off.

What can you do to make sure the prisoners do not try to escape while the force field is down?

36. Mexican Laser Standoff
(solution on page 70)

You are a cyborg in a duel with two other cyborgs. You have a laser beam attached to your arm that fires with 33% accuracy. One of the other cyborgs shoots with 50% accuracy, and the other shoots with 100% accuracy. Each of you is allowed one shot per round and the shooting order starts from the worst shooter to the best shooter. You will shoot first, the 50% accurate cyborg will shoot second, and the 100% accurate cyborg will shoot third. If a cyborg is killed, their turn will be skipped. You, having the worst shot, are up first.

What should you shoot at to maximize your chance of winning?

37. A Duck In The Pond
(solution on page 71)

You have two pets that you have recently purchased from the market, a duck and a wolf. The duck is sitting in the center of the circular pond in your backyard and the wolf is standing at the edge of the water ready to eat the duck.

If the wolf runs four times as fast as the duck can swim and the duck cannot fly until it has its feet on solid ground, how can the duck make it to the edge of the pond to fly away without being eaten by the wolf?

38. Racehorses
(solution on page 72)

You own a farm and have raised 25 racehorses. Each horse runs at a different but constant pace. When the horses race they will always run at the same pace no matter how many times they race. You are trying to find your three fastest horses. You do not have a clock of any kind to time the horses, and you can only race five horses against each other at a time.

What is the minimum number of races you need to conduct in order to find your three fastest racehorses?

39. A Dozen Weighted Balls
(solution on page 73)

You have a dozen identical-looking balls and a balance scale. One of these balls has a slightly different weight from all of the others. What is the minimum amount of times you need to use the balance scale to determine which ball has the unique weight and whether it is heavier or lighter than the others?

40. <u>Two Cups And A Bucket</u>
(solution on page 75)

You have two small cups filled with water and an empty bucket. How can you dump all of the water out of the cups and into the bucket and tell which water came from which cup without using any dividers of any sort?

41. <u>Don't Marry That One!</u>
(solution on page 76)

You have been brought up in a family that does arranged marriages and you are being forced to marry one of three sisters. One of the sisters always tells the truth, one of the sisters always lies, and the other will sometimes lie and sometimes tell the truth. You do not know which sister is which but you do know that the sister that sometimes lies and sometimes tells the truth has an awful disease that you will catch if you marry her.

You don't like any of the sisters and are content with marrying either the truth-teller or the liar but you absolutely do not want to marry the diseased sister.

If the three sisters are standing next to each other, can you approach one sister and ask her a yes or no question that will guarantee you can make a safe decision regarding which sister you are going to marry?

42. <u>King Arthur's Coin Game</u>
(solution on page 77)

You are with King Arthur at his perfectly round table. You each have a huge pile of gold coins and have agreed to play a game. The winner gets to keep all of the gold. The rules are as follows: each player will in turn place a coin on the table. The coin must lay flat, it cannot overlap any other coins, and it cannot hang off the edge of the table. The first player unable to successfully place a coin loses. King Arthur thinks he's really good at this game and has decided to let you go first.

What strategy can you come up with the guarantee that you win?

43. The Bronx vs. Brooklyn
(solution on page 78)

There is a young man who lives in Manhattan near a subway station. He has two girlfriends; one lives in Brooklyn and the other lives in The Bronx. To visit the girl in Brooklyn he must take the train heading downtown, and to visit the girl that lives in The Bronx he must take the train heading uptown. The young man likes both girls equally and decides that he is going to just get on the first train that comes to the platform and let chance decide which girlfriend he visits. Each train arrives at the station every ten minutes and the man arrives at the platform at a random time every morning. Despite these conditions, the man finds himself spending nine out of ten days with the girlfriend that lives in The Bronx.

Why is this happening?

44. Three Playing Cards
(solution on page 79)

In front of you are three ordinary playing cards arranged in a horizontal row. To the right of the Jack there's at least one King. To the left of that King there's at least one King. To the left of the Club there's at least one Heart. To the right of the Heart there's at least one Heart. What are the three playing cards and what order are they in?

45. Colored Weights
(solution on page 80)

You have a balance scale and six weights. There are two red weights, two white weights, and two blue weights. In each pair of colored weights one weight is slightly heavier than the other but is otherwise identical. The three heavier weights all weigh the same and the three lighter weights all weigh the same.

What is the fewest number of times you need to use the balance scale in order to positively identify the heavier weight in each pair?

46. Calendar Cubes
(solution on page 81)

A businessman has two regular cubes on his office desk. Each cube has six single-digit numbers on it. Every day he arranges both cubes so that the front faces show the current day of the month. What are the numbers on each face of each cube?

47. Finding Your Seat
(solution on page 82)

You are running late in an airport and are in the very back of the line to board your plane. The plane seats fifty people. The first person in line forgot his seat number and chooses a seat at random when he enters the plane. Each subsequent person will sit in their assigned seat unless it is taken by someone else. If they find their seat already occupied, they will choose another seat at random.

If you are the last person to board the plane, what is the probability that you will get your assigned seat?

48. Three Prospective Employees
(solution on page 83)

Three perfectly intelligent men, Alan, Bob, and Cal, are applying for the same job position. They are equally capable and the employer is having a hard time deciding which man to hire. He decides to play a simple game and give the job to the first person that solves it:

A black or white hat is placed on each man's head and each man can see the other men's hats but not their own. They are instructed to raise their hands if they see a black hat and the first person to tell the employer what color hat they are wearing and how they figured this out will get the job. After the hats are placed on Alan, Bob, and Cal's heads, each man raises his hand. After a few seconds, Alan says: "I've figured it out!"

What color hat is Alan wearing and how did he know?

49. Late To Work
(solution on page 84)

Just as Alan is about to be hired, Dan walks into the room late for the interview. The employer had already taken a liking to Dan and wanted to give him a chance too so he decides to play another very similar game, now with four players:

A black or white hat is placed on each man's head and each man can see the other men's hats but not their own. They are instructed this time to raise their hands if they see at least two black hats and the first person to tell the employer what color hat they are wearing and how they figured this out will get the job. After the hats are placed on Alan, Bob, Cal, and Dan's heads, each man raises his hand. After a few seconds, Alan says once more: "I've figured it out!"

What color hat is Alan wearing and how did he know?

50. Intellectuals Standing In Line With Hats
(solution on page 85)

Four perfectly intelligent men, Alan, Bob, Cal, and Dan, who have taken quite a liking to solving problems with hats, are standing in a single file line. Alan is in the back of the line and standing in front of him are Bob, Cal, and Dan, in that order. A hat is placed on each man's head and each of the four hats is one of three different colors: red, white, or blue. There is at least one hat of each color on the men's heads. The men cannot see the color of their own hat but can see the hats of each man standing in front of them in line. Alan can see Bob, Cal, and Dan's hats. Bob can see Cal and Dan's hats. Cal can see Dan's hat. Dan cannot see anyone's hat. Starting with Alan, each man is asked if they know the color of their hat and, if they do know, to announce which color hat they are wearing. Each man can hear each answer. Strangely enough, Alan, Bob, Cal, and Dan are all able to deduce and announce the color of their hats correctly.

How were the hats arranged so that this situation was possible without any one of them having to guess? How did they each deduce the color of their hat?

51. Numbered Foreheads
(solution on page 86)

You are in a room with two perfectly intelligent men, Eugene and Frank, and a painter, Claude. Claude has painted a unique number on each of your foreheads. Each number is a whole number greater than zero, and one of the numbers is the sum of the other two. You, Eugene, and Frank know this information. You see the number "20" painted on Eugene's head and the number "30" painted on Frank's forehead. Claude then asks you, "do you know what your number is, and if so, what is it?" You reply "no" because at this point it is impossible for you to deduce which number you have painted on your forehead. Claude then asks Eugene the same question, to which Eugene also replies, "no." Claude then asks Frank the same question, to which he also replies, "no." Claude then turns to you and asks once more, "do you know what your number is, and if so, what is it?"

How do you respond this time?

52. Rope Burning
(solution on page 87)

You have a lighter and two ropes. Each rope takes one hour to burn completely. Both ropes have varying thicknesses, meaning that different parts of each rope burn at different speeds. How can you accurately time forty-five minutes with just the two ropes and the lighter?

53. A Stopped Watch
(solution on page 88)

A watch that runs normally but is out-of-sync will not be right more than a few times over the course of a month. A stopped watch will be right two times a day. A clever old man adjusted his watch so that it gives the correct time at least twice a day and still runs at the normal rate. Assuming he didn't know what time it was and was not able to set the watch perfectly, what did the clever old man do?

54. Hotel Security
(solution on page 89)

Alan and Bob are staying in two different rooms in the same hotel. Alan has a valuable ring that he wants to give to Bob, but an unbelievable set of circumstances have led to spies lurking around the hotel trying to find and kill both Alan and Bob. Because of this neither of them are able to safely leave their room. The only way they are able to transfer items to and from each other is with the help of the bellhops that work at the hotel. Alan and Bob each have a small portable safe that can be secured with multiple locks. Alan and Bob each have a padlock and corresponding key. Unfortunately, the bellhops are thieves and will steal anything and everything that is inside of the safes if they are unlocked.

How can Alan securely send the valuable ring to Bob without it being stolen?

55. The Secret Of Monk Island
(solution on page 90)

There is a small island full of perfectly intelligent monks where everyone has either brown or blue eyes. The monks that have blue eyes are believed to be cursed and are required to commit suicide at midnight. However, the monks have all taken a vow and no one is allowed to tell anyone what color eyes they have. The island has no reflective surfaces and there is absolutely no way for any of the monks to know the color of their own eyes; they are only able to see the eyes of everyone else on the island. Because of this, life on the island goes on uninterrupted and no one ever commits suicide.

One day a man who was lost at sea arrives on the shore of the island in a boat. All of the monks run to the shore to see who the man is, and the man says to them, "At least one of you has blue eyes!" After hearing this new information the monks all panic and look around at each other.

What happens that night at midnight?

56. Flipping Quarters
(solution on page 91)

There is a table in front of you with one hundred quarters on it. You have been blindfolded and are wearing a thick pair of gloves. You are not able to see whether the quarters are heads or tails because you are blindfolded and you are not able to feel whether the quarters are heads or tails because of the thick gloves. Your friend tells you that twenty of these quarters are tails and the remaining eighty are heads, but you do not know which are which. He tells you that if you are able to split the quarters into two piles where the number of tails quarters is the same in each pile you will win all of the quarters. You are free to move the quarters and flip them over and arrange them into two piles of any amount.

Without knowing which quarters are heads and which are tails, what can you do to win this game?

57. Truth, Falsehood, Randomness
(solution on page 92)

Standing in front of you are three men. One man always tells the truth, one man always lies, and the other man always answers questions randomly. The three men all know which one of them is which, but you do not. With only three yes or no questions how can you determine who is who?

58. <u>The Stolen Blue Carbuncle</u>

(solution on page 94)

A famous blue carbuncle has been stolen! An eyewitness saw someone steal this gem out of the museum but is not able to give any sort of description. There is no physical evidence of the crime. A group of Scotland Yard detectives suspect that one of the three most notorious jewel thieves in the area might be responsible. All three of these suspects are taken into custody but there is not enough evidence to arrest any of them. Each of these three suspects denies taking the blue carbuncle. The three jewel thieves were having dinner together after being released from custody and were being watched by a surveillance team.

At one time or another during dinner, each man got up to use the bathroom. While each man was in the bathroom, the other two thieves at the table flipped a coin in private. Neither the surveillance team nor the thief in the bathroom was able to see any coin flips or their results. After the last thief returned from the bathroom, the three of them all winked at each other and left in silence. The surveillance team saw only the back of one thief's head when he winked, so his wink was not recorded.

The surveillance team is certain that all three thieves now know whether or not one of them stole the Blue Carbuncle. However, the thieves, even if they are sure that one of them did steal it, do not know exactly who did it and the surveillance team does not even know whether or not one of the thieves is guilty.

How was all of this information communicated?

59. Three Locks
(solution on page 95)

Three thieves rob a bank and go back to their hideout. They take the stolen money and put it in a safe with a locked security door on it. The door is fitted with three locks, each controlled by a button next to it. All three locks are initially deactivated and once a lock becomes activated there is no way to tell whether or not it is locked. Pressing a button will activate the corresponding deactivated lock or deactivate the corresponding activated lock. The three thieves want to work out a system so that any two of them can open the safe and access the money but a single thief cannot open the door on his own. If a thief tries to open the safe door and all three locks aren't deactivated an alarm will sound and alert the other two thieves. Also, each thief is only allowed to give information about which locks he toggled to one other thief.

What is a system that they can come up with to allow for this to work?

60. Bear Hunting
(solution on page 96)

A famous hunter woke up early one morning and headed south to hunt bears after he finished eating his breakfast. After travelling a mile south he spotted a bear, aimed his gun, fired, and missed. The bear got scared and started heading east. The hunter followed the bear and caught up with it after travelling half of a mile. He shot the bear this time but only wounded it. The bear limped on towards the east again and after another half of a mile the hunter finally shot and killed the beast. The hunter then walked the mile north back to his cabin and found it being ransacked by another bear.

What color is the bear that was tearing up the hunter's cabin?

61. <u>Blind Men's Socks</u>
(solution on page 97)

A blind man is leaving a store in the mall with three pairs of black socks and three pairs of white socks. Each pair of socks is rubber-banded together. As he is leaving the store another blind man is walking into the store with an identical three pairs of black socks and three pairs of white socks that he wants to return. These pairs of socks are also rubber-banded together. As the two blind men cross paths they accidentally bump into each other and drop all of their socks. They apologize to one another and within a few minutes, despite being totally blind and without the help of anyone else, have everything sorted back out and they each end up with three pairs of black socks and three pairs of white socks.

How did the blind men do this?

62. <u>Five Greedy Pirates</u>
(solution on page 98)

There are five perfectly intelligent and greedy pirates. They have one hundred gold coins to split between the five of them. The pirates have seniority in the following order: Pirate A, Pirate B, Pirate C, Pirate D, then Pirate E. Each pirate knows the rules of the game they are about to play, which goes as follows: Pirate A makes a suggestion about how to split up the coins (for example, he can say that he gets fifty coins, Pirate B gets ten coins, Pirate C gets ten coins, Pirate D gets ten coins, and Pirate E gets twenty coins). All of the pirates, including Pirate A, then vote on the suggested allocation. If there is a majority of votes or a tic for the suggestion then the allocation is approved and the game ends. Otherwise, Pirate A is thrown off of the boat to his death and Pirate B becomes the most senior pirate and gets to make his own suggestion. The game continues in this fashion until an agreement is reached.

Considering that all five of these pirates are perfectly intelligent and greedy, what will Pirate A propose to everyone?

63. Stealing Bell Ropes

(solution on page 99)

You are locked in a room that is fifty feet wide by fifty feet long with a one hundred foot tall ceiling. You are a skilled acrobat and you are carrying a sharp knife. Attached to the ceiling are two hooks that are two feet apart, and tied to each hook is a one hundred foot long rope. Each rope hangs all the way down to the ground. There is nothing in the room to stand on and if you fall from any higher than twenty feet you will die.

Using only your climbing skills and your knife, how much of the two hundred feet of rope can you acquire while ending up safe on the ground?

64. Three Coins

(solution on page 100)

Your friend wants to play a game. You are to turn your back as your friend places three coins, a nickel, a dime, and a quarter on a table behind you. He can arrange them in any pattern of heads or tails as long as they are not all the same. You then tell your friend to flip the coins any way you would like. For example, you can say "flip the dime" or "flip all three coins", etc. Your goal is to get all three coins to be the same, either all heads or all tails. As soon as all three coins are the same, your friend will tell you that you've won.

What is the best strategy to use to win the game in the fewest number of steps possible?

65. <u>Two Trees And An Island</u>
(solution on page 101)

You are standing at the edge of a lake. The lake is five hundred feet in diameter and there is a small island directly in the middle. There is a large tree next to you and a large tree in the middle of the island. You cannot swim and you have a little over five hundred feet in rope. How can you use the rope as a means to get to the island in the middle of the lake?

66. <u>A Camel & Bananas</u>
(solution on page 102)

You are a banana salesman stranded in the desert with your camel. There is a town that is one thousand miles away. You have three thousand bananas and your camel can only carry a thousand bananas at a time. The camel is very stubborn and will only move a mile before you have to feed it one of the bananas to make it move another mile. What is the maximum amount of uneaten bananas that you can transport to the town?

67. <u>Trapped In A Room</u>
(solution on page 103)

You are trapped in a very small room. In the middle of each side of the room there is a hole with a button inside. The button can either be on or off but you cannot see in the holes and cannot feel whether the button is on or off. You can stick your hands in any two of these four holes at a time and either push both buttons, push one button, or do nothing. The goal is to set all four buttons to the same state, whether they are all on or all off. If you are successful, the room will open up and you can escape. You will not know if you have succeeded until you remove both of your hands from the holes. However, if you remove both of your hands from the holes and you have not succeeded in setting all of the buttons to the same state, the room will spin around very quickly and disorient you so that you cannot tell which wall is which.

How do you put all of the buttons into the same position and escape from the room?

68. Past, Present, & Future
(solution on page 104)

You are in a chamber with three gods: Past, Present, and Future. The three gods all look identical to one another and you cannot distinguish one from another. The gods all answer any questions truthfully, but with these conditions: Past answers the last question asked in the chamber, Present answers the question currently being asked, and Future answers the next question that will be asked in the chamber. Additionally, the gods speak a language that you cannot fully understand. Instead of answering "yes" or "no" they answer "da" and "ya" but you aren't sure which means which.

By coming up with three questions, which must all be determined ahead of time because of Past and Future, how do you determine which god is which?

69. Figuring Out Numbers
(solution on page 105)

Alan and Bob, two perfectly intelligent mathematicians, are trying to figure out two different numbers. They know that both numbers are integers between 1 and 100. They also know that neither of the numbers are 1 or 100. Alan knows only the product of the numbers and Bob knows only the sum of the numbers. Alan says to Bob, "I cannot tell what the two numbers are." Bob replies, "I already knew you couldn't." Alan then says, "Ah, now I know the numbers!" Bob replies enthusiastically, "Now I know them too!"

What must the two numbers be?

70. The Switchers

(solution on page 107)

There are five men in front of you. One of them is a truth-teller, a man who always tells the truth, and four of them are what are called "Switchers" that behave in the following way: The first time you ask them a question they will answer with either the truth or a lie, randomly. The second time you ask them a question, they will answer in the opposite way of how they answered for the first question. So if they answer the first question truthfully, they will answer the second question with a lie, the third question truthfully, the fourth question with a lie, and so on and so forth.

By asking only two questions (each question can only be directed to one person at a time), how can you determine which of the five men in front of you is the truth-teller?

71. Making Ice

(solution on page 108)

On a table in front of you is a small freezer that is capable of holding seven standard ice cube trays stacked on top of each other. There are no shelves to separate the trays, and if you stack one tray on top of another before the ice cubes in the bottom tray are fully frozen, the top tray will sink into the bottom tray and you will not be able to make full-sized ice cubes. You have an unlimited supply of trays, each of which can make a dozen ice cubes.

If it takes fifteen minutes for the water to freeze completely into an ice cube, what is the maximum amount of full-sized ice cubes you can produce in sixty minutes?

72. The Blue Forehead Room
(solution on page 109)

There are one hundred perfectly intelligent logicians enclosed in a room and standing in a circle. They have all gotten their foreheads painted some color and are unable to see the color of their own forehead but can see the forehead of every other person in the room. They are told that at least one of them has their forehead painted blue and that if you are able to deduce that you have a blue forehead you are to leave the room after the lights have been turned off. The person in charge of painting the foreheads has decided to paint everyone's forehead blue.

If the lights get turned on and off a total of one hundred times, what will happen each time?

73. The Game Show
(solution on page 111)

You are a contestant on a game show. There are three closed doors in front of you. The game show host tells you that behind one of these doors is a million dollars in cash and that behind the other two doors there are goats. You do not know which doors contain which prizes but the game show host does.

The game you are going to play is very simple: you pick one of the three doors and win the prize behind it. After you have made your selection, the game show host opens one of the two doors that you did not choose and reveals a goat. At this point you are given the option to either stick with your original door or switch your choice to the only remaining closed door.

What would you do and why?

74. <u>One Hundred Prisoners & Two Light Bulbs</u>
(solution on page 112)

One hundred prisoners are imprisoned in solitary cells. Each cell is soundproofed and totally windowless. There is a central living room with two light bulbs that are initially off. No prisoner can see the light bulbs from their own cell. The warden decides he is going to play a game with all of the prisoners. If they win they will all be let free, but if they lose the game they will all be immediately executed.

The game works as follows: Each day the warden will pick a prisoner's name at random out of a hat, put the prisoners name back in the hat, and then take that prisoner to the central room. After spending fifteen minutes in the room the prisoner will be escorted back to their cell. While they are in the room the prisoner is allowed to toggle either of the light bulbs on or off as they choose. The prisoner also has the option to tell the warden "All one hundred of us have been taken to this room since this game has started." If the prisoner is correct the game is over and the prisoners win. If the prisoner is wrong and this statement is incorrect the game ends and all of the prisoners are executed. Thus, this statement should only be made if the prisoner is absolutely certain that they are correct. Before the game begins all one hundred of the prisoners are allowed to get together in the courtyard and discuss a plan.

What is the best plan that the prisoners can come up with so that eventually someone will be able to make a correct assertion and win the game, granting them all freedom?

75. A Dozen Hatted Prisoners

(solution on page 114)

Twelve straightjacketed prisoners are on death row. Tomorrow they will be arranged in a single-file line, positions determined randomly, all facing the same direction. The person in the back of the line, who will be referred to as the twelfth person, can see the eleven people standing in front of him; the eleventh person can see the ten people standing in front of him, but not the twelfth person who is standing behind him; so on and so forth until you get to the first person in line who cannot see anyone. The warden of this prison likes to play games with his prisoners and has lined everyone up in this fashion so that he can give them an opportunity to gain their freedom.

The warden will place, at random, a black or white hat on each prisoner's head. The prisoners cannot see the color of the hat they are wearing, but they can see the color of the hats of each prisoner standing in front of them in line. After all of the hats have been placed on the prisoners' heads, the warden asks the person in the back of the line, the twelfth person, "what is the color of the hat on your head?" The prisoner can reply by saying either "black" or "white" but nothing else. When the prisoner answers the warden, all of the prisoners in line can hear the reply but they do not know whether the prisoner was right or wrong. If the prisoner replies with the correct color of their hat they will be freed from the prison. If they are wrong they will be executed that night. This game continues until all twelve of the prisoners in line have been asked about the color of their hat. While the game is in progress no prisoner is allowed to speak, move, or do anything until it is their turn to answer the question. The warden allows the prisoners to get together in the courtyard the day before this game begins to come up with a plan to maximize the number of lives they can save.

What is the prisoners' plan?

76. Einstein's Riddle

(solution on page 115)

Somewhere in the world there is a small neighborhood full of very eccentric and intelligent people. There are five houses that are each a different color. There is a person of a different nationality that lives in each house. Each of these five people drinks their own special drink, smokes their own special brand of cigarettes, and has their own special pet. No one has the same pet, smokes the same brand of cigarettes, or drinks the same drink. One of these five people owns a pet fish. With just the following information, figure out who owns the fish:

The British man lives in the red house.

The Swedish man has a dog for a pet.

The Danish man drinks tea.

The green house is to the left of the white house.

The owner of the green house drinks coffee.

The person that smokes Pall Mall cigarettes has a bird.

The owner of the yellow house smokes Dunhill cigarettes.

The person that lives in the middle house drinks milk.

The Norwegian lives in the first house.

The person that smokes Blend cigarettes lives next to the one that has a cat.

The person that has a horse lives next to the one that smokes Dunhill cigarettes.

The one that smokes Bluemaster cigarettes drinks beer.

The German smokes Prince cigarettes.

The Norwegian lives next to a blue house.

The person that smokes Blend cigarettes has a neighbor that drinks water.

77. The Impossible Rainbow

(solution on page 116)

Seven prisoners are on death row. Tomorrow all seven of them will be randomly arranged in a circle and they will each have a hat put on their head by the warden. Each hat may be any one of the seven colors of the rainbow (red, orange, yellow, green, blue, indigo, or violet) and the hats will be distributed randomly. There is a large enough supply of hats so that it is possible for each of the seven prisoners to be wearing the same color hat. It is also possible for each prisoner to be wearing a different color hat. Each prisoner can see the hats of the six other prisoners in the circle, but they cannot see their own hat.

The warden tells them all that he will play a game and offer them their collective freedom as a prize. Each prisoner is given a slip of paper and writes down his guess of his own hat color. After all of the prisoners have finished, the warden will look at each slip of paper and if at least one prisoner has guessed the correct color of his hat they will all be set free. If none of the prisoners have written down the color of their own hat, they will all be executed immediately. If the prisoners communicate in any way while this game is being played, they will all be executed immediately. The warden allows the prisoners to get together in the courtyard the day before this game begins to come up with a plan.

What strategy do the prisoners come up with to guarantee that they will be set free?

78. One Hundred Prisoners & One Hundred Boxes

(solution on page 117)

One hundred extremely intelligent prisoners are imprisoned in solitary cells and on death row. Each cell is soundproofed and completely windowless. There is a room with one hundred small boxes numbered and labeled from 1 to 100. Inside each of these boxes is a slip of paper with one of the prisoners' names on it. Each prisoner's name only appears once and is in only one of the hundred boxes. The warden decides he is going to play a game with all of the prisoners. If they win they will all be let free, but if they lose the game they will all be immediately executed.

The hundred prisoners are allowed to enter this room in any predetermined order they wish but each can only enter the room once and the game ends as soon as the hundredth person enters the room. Once they enter the room, the prisoners are each allowed to open and look inside any fifty boxes. After they have opened the fifty boxes and looked inside, they must shut them and leave everything exactly the way it was before they entered. The prisoners are not allowed to communicate with each other in any way. If every prisoner is able to enter the room and open the box that contains his own name, they will all be released from prison immediately! However, if even just one prisoner enters the room, opens fifty boxes, and does not open the box containing his own name, they will all be executed immediately. Luckily for the prisoners the warden has decided to allow the first prisoner in the room to open all one hundred boxes and switch any two names if they would like to.

Again, in order to win this game, all one hundred prisoners need to enter the room and open the box with their name in it. The warden allows the prisoners to get together in the courtyard the week before this game begins to come up with a plan.

What strategy do the prisoners come up with to guarantee that they win this game?

THE SOLUTIONS

1. <u>Redmond's Question</u>

SOLUTION

This famous riddle has a few equally famous answers. It was made famous by Microsoft when they started including this question in some interviews. It was asked to see how prospective employees would answer a question with multiple answers in order to try and better understand the type of thinkers and problem-solvers the people were. Here are a few of the most popular answers to this question:

♦ Round manhole covers cannot fall through the circular opening, where a square manhole cover may fall in if it is inserted diagonally.

♦ Round manhole covers do not need to be rotated to a certain position in order to fit in place.

♦ Round manhole covers are easy to move because they do not necessarily need to be carried, they can be rolled like a wheel.

There are infinite answers to this question - which is why it is a great interview question and a great way to get your mind working.

2. Eating Garbage

SOLUTION

Your friend's favorite food is corn on the cob. You throw away the husk, cook the corn that is inside, then eat the outside of the corn and throw away the core that is inside.

3. Fox Trotting

SOLUTION

A fox can only run halfway into the woods. Any further and he will be running *out* of the woods.

Please note: this riddle's wordplay is not representative of any of the problems that follow it. It was included to set the mood and as an example of a problem with an out-of-the-box solution.

4. <u>Fork In The Road</u>

SOLUTION

To make sure you choose the correct path, you can ask one of the two men the following question: "Which road would the other guy tell me to take in order to get to my destination?"

If this question is asked to the truth-teller he will tell the truth and tell you the path that the liar would tell you to go down, which would be a lie and the incorrect path. If this question is asked to the liar he will lie and tell you that the truth-teller would tell you to take the path that is the wrong direction.

So, if you ask this question to either the truth-teller or the liar, you simply go the opposite direction that they tell you and you will reach your destination.

5. River Dilemma

SOLUTION

To make it across the other side of the river without losing any of the items you just purchased at the market, you can make the following trips:

- Bring the duck over.

- Return alone.

- Bring the wolf over.

- Return with the duck.

- Bring the bag of seeds over.

- Return alone.

- Bring the duck over.

Now you'll be on the other side of the river with all three purchases and able to make it back home safely.

6. Circular Divisions

SOLUTION

Many people will first split the circle into nine sections, then quickly they'll make it to ten sections, and eventually some people will make it to eleven sections, which is the maximum number. There are obviously many ways to split the circle into eleven sections, but here is one solution:

Take the circle and imagine it as a clock face. Draw a line from the twelve to the six, the two to the seven, the three to the nine, and then the final line goes from the five to a place in between the eleven and twelve. This results in eleven sections:

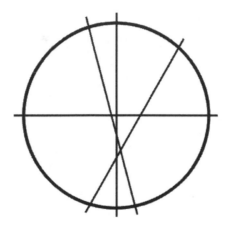

7. <u>French Toasting</u>

SOLUTION

You can make three perfect slices of French toast in only a minute and a half. Label each of the three slices of bread: Slice 1, Slice 2, and Slice 3.

- ◆   First, put Slice 1 and Slice 2 in the frying pan for thirty seconds.

- ◆   Then, take Slice 1 out of the pan, put Slice 3 in the pan, and flip Slice 2 over for thirty more seconds.

- ◆   In the last thirty seconds you take the perfectly cooked Slice 2 out of the pan, flip Slice 3 over, and put Slice 1 back in with the uncooked side face-down.

Now you will have three perfectly cooked pieces of French toast that you can enjoy in only a minute and a half.

8. <u>Flipping Two Coins</u>

SOLUTION

There are four possible outcomes when you flip two coins: heads & heads, tails & tails, heads & tails, or tails & heads. Because at least one of the coins is tails, that leaves you with only three possible outcomes. Out of these three outcomes only one of them satisfies the condition of both coins coming up tails, therefore the probability for both coins being tails is 1/3.

9. Nuts, Bolts, Nuts & Bolts

SOLUTION

The key to this riddle is the fact that all of the boxes are labeled incorrectly.

The way to correctly label all of the boxes with only one selection is to reach into the box labeled "Nuts & Bolts" and pull something out. Suppose you pull out a bolt, which means that that box must be "Bolts", you now know that the remaining two boxes are "Nuts" and "Nuts & Bolts" but since the "Nuts" box is labeled incorrectly it must be the "Nuts & Bolts" and the "Bolts" box then must actually be "Nuts".

10. Cake Slicing

SOLUTION

This is a personal favorite of mine because it is so easy to remember and tell people, and everyone is capable of solving it. You can make eight equal sized slices in three cuts:

- ◆ First cut the cake straight down the middle splitting it into two pieces.

- ◆ Then cut straight down the middle of those two pieces to make four equal pieces.

- ◆ Then make a horizontal cut across the center of the cake to split those four pieces into eight.

11. Halfway Glass

SOLUTION

The most accurate way to determine whether the glass is half-full, more than half-full, or less than half-full is by tilting the glass sideways until the water touches the lip of the glass. Because the glass is a right cylinder, you can look at where the water towards the bottom of the glass is to determine how much water there is. If the water perfectly intersects the corner of the bottom of the glass it is half-full. If the water level at the bottom of the glass is above the corner, the glass is more than half-full. And if the water level at the bottom of the glass is below the corner, the glass is less than half-full.

12. A Hanging Chain

SOLUTION

This riddle is nothing more than a simple math problem. If the chain is four feet long and it is hanging vertically a distance of two feet, it must be hanging perfectly straight, meaning that the distance between the two nails is zero. Realistically, all this means is that both nails are going through both ends of the chain.

13. The Loaded Coin

SOLUTION

This riddle has a few solutions. Technically there are infinite ways you can flip an unfair coin and determine a winner based solely on chance but it requires the rules to become more and more complex as you come up with new solutions. I will provide the three most elegant answers.

The most famous answer for this problem is using a strategy commonly attributed to the mathematician John Von Neumann. To construct a fair game of chance with an unbiased coin that flips heads more than tails, all you need to do is follow these rules: Flip the coin twice. If it comes up heads and then tails, you win. If it comes up tails and then heads, your best friend wins. If it comes up heads and then heads, or tails and then tails, you start over. The two instances of heads-then-tails and tails-then-heads are equally probably, regardless of how unbalanced the coin is. This provides a fair contest.

Another answer is for you and your best friend to each flip the coin ten times. Whoever flips more heads wins. If you tie, you start over. This answer demonstrates the ease in which you can come up with infinite solutions by slightly changing the rules for a contest like this.

One more answer is to say to your friend, "We will each flip the coin as many times as it takes to flip tails. Whoever can do this in the least amount of flips wins." This is also a fair contest.

14. <u>Who Makes What?</u>

SOLUTION

This is another riddle with multiple solutions. One way to determine the average salary without disclosing any individual's salary is to have each person write two numbers on two slips of paper that when averaged together equal their salary. For example, the first person could write $10,000 on one slip of paper and $60,000 on another slip of paper if he made $35,000. After each person has done this, they put all six of the slips into a hat and mix them all around. Then one of them draws all six slips out of the hat and takes an average of all of them to come up with the average salary of the three people.

Another solution, which eliminates the possibility of handwriting recognition that may bias the first answer, is for one of the three people to come up with a random number in his head. He will then add his salary to that number and write the sum on a slip of paper and pass it to another person. This person then adds their salary to the number and writes the new number on a slip and passes it to the third person. The third person adds their salary to the new number and then writes this down on a slip and hands it back to the first person. The first person then subtracts his random number and divides the remainder by three to come up with the average salary of all three people.

15. Water Buckets

SOLUTION

First, completely fill the 5-gallon bucket. Then pour the 5-gallon bucket into the 3-gallon bucket until you fill the 3-gallon bucket completely. This leaves two gallons of water in the 5-gallon bucket. Then dump out the 3-gallon bucket and pour the two gallons of water into it. Now fill the empty 5-gallon bucket back up using the faucet and pour the 5-gallon bucket into the 3-gallon bucket until the 3-gallon bucket is full. This will take one gallon's worth of water, leaving you with four gallons of water in the 5-gallon bucket.

16. <u>Prison Escape</u>

SOLUTION

All the man is trying to do is dig enough into the floor to make a pile of dirt large enough for him to stand on and reach the skylight.

17. <u>The Dove In The Hand</u>

SOLUTION

The wise man knew better than to answer the boys' question because all the boys have to do is bring a live dove with them and they can easily trick him: If he says the dove is alive, they will kill the bird behind their backs and show him a dead bird, and if he says the dove is dead, they will simply show him the live dove. Stupid kids.

18. <u>Stones, Jars, Life, Death</u>

SOLUTION

The best chance at survival comes with a distribution as follows: Put one white stone in the first jar, and all of the remaining stones in the other. This provides you with a 74.74% chance of survival.

19. Immanuel The Clock Setter

SOLUTION

This is what Immanuel did to reset his clock: First, he wound his clock up before he left and set it to twelve-o-clock. Then he traveled to his friend's house and noted the time on his friend's clock when he walked in. Before he left, he noted the time on the clock once again. He made sure to remember the duration of time he spent at the house. He walked home and noted the time on his grandfather clock. The difference in time between what his grandfather clock read when he walked in and the twelve-o-clock time it was set to when he left is the total duration of time he spent on his trip. He subtracted the time he spent at his friend's house from this time, which gives him the amount of time he spent on his walk to-and-from the friend's house. To set his clock correctly, he must take half of this number and add it to the time the clock at his friend's house said when he was on his way out. Now he'll have the correct time.

20. The Coin Flipping Game

SOLUTION

A coin is a very simply probability device if it is flipped one time. The more coins you flip, the more times you flip them, and the more rules you add to the coins makes their simplicity magically vanish.

There is a 3.9% chance that you will play this game one time and win exactly eight dollars from your friend. Perhaps think of it like this: To win eight dollars the game must end on the eighth flip. There are two hundred and fifty-six different ways for eight coin flips to turn out. For the game to end on the eighth flip there needs to have been four heads flipped and four tails flipped. But the game also has opportunities to end on the second, fourth, and sixth flip. Because of this, we can rule out every eight-flip sequence whose first two flips contain one heads and one tails. We can also rule out every eight-flip sequence whose first four flips contain two heads and two tails and we can rule out every eight-flip sequence whose first six flips contains three heads and three tails.

After ruling all of these sequences out, there are only ten sequences that remain that will result in the game ending on the eighth flip. With only ten acceptable sequences out of two hundred and fifty-six possibilities you wind up with a 3.9% chance of winning exactly eight dollars.

21. The Scale Of All Scales

SOLUTION

You would only need five weights in order to do this. There are multiple configurations, but one solution is a set of the following weights (in pounds): 1, 3, 9, 27, and 60. The key to this riddle is to understand that you can weigh something that weighs two pounds by putting the object and the one-pound weight on one side of the scale and the three-pound weight on the other side. Once this 'clicks' in your mind you realize how few weights you need to be able to count all the way up to 100.

22. <u>Something Wicked Which Way Comes?</u>

SOLUTION

All Jim needs to do to determine if he is headed the right way is to ask the person another question that he knows will be answered with a yes. Jim can ask, "Did I just ask you a question?" and if the person rubs their stomach Jim knows that that means "yes" and he knows he is headed in the right direction. If he asks them that question and they do something else he knows he is headed in the wrong direction because whatever action they respond with must mean "yes" and thus he can be sure that the stomach rubbing did not.

23. <u>Water Buckets II</u>

SOLUTION

Dividing the twelve gallons of water equally into two buckets can be done in seven steps:

- ◆ Pour the 12-gallon bucket into the 8-gallon bucket.

- ◆ Pour the 8-gallon bucket into the 5-gallon bucket. You now have four gallons in the 12-gallon bucket, three gallons in the 8-gallon bucket, and five gallons in the 5-gallon bucket.

- ◆ Pour the 5-gallon bucket into the 12-gallon bucket.

- ◆ Pour the 8-gallon bucket into the 5-gallon bucket. You now have nine gallons in the 12-gallon bucket, nothing in the 8-gallon bucket, and three gallons in the 5-gallon bucket.

- ◆ Pour the 12-gallon bucket into the 8-gallon bucket, the 8-gallon bucket into the 5-gallon bucket, and the 5-gallon bucket into the 12-gallon bucket.

This will leave you with exactly six gallons of water in the 12-gallon bucket and exactly six gallons of water in the 8-gallon bucket.

24. Making Change

SOLUTION

The maximum value of change you can have without being able to give exact change for a dollar is $1.19 - this is achievable in two ways: The first way is with three quarters, four dimes, and four pennies. The second way is with one quarter, nine dimes, and four pennies.

25. <u>Race To The Finish</u>

SOLUTION

The wise old man says to his sons: "Why don't you boys just switch and ride each other's horses?"

26. <u>Five Hats In A Box</u>

SOLUTION

The only configuration that would allow for this situation is if Bob and Cal are both wearing black hats. If Alan were to see two white hats in front of him, he would be able to deduce that he is wearing a black hat because there are only two white hats in the box. In all other instances he must respond with a "no". If Bob were to see a white hat in front of him he would be able to deduce that he was wearing a black hat because he would know that both him and Cal couldn't be wearing white hats otherwise Alan would have known the color of his hat. Because of all this, Alan and Bob do not know the color of their hats and Cal can be sure about the color of his own hat, which is black.

27. Weighing Fake Coins

SOLUTION

You can find the counterfeit coins with only one weighing. Because you know that the real coins weigh an ounce each and the counterfeit coins weigh half an ounce each, this is what you can do:

Take one coin from the first group, two coins from the second group, three coins from the third group, and continue in this fashion until you get to the tenth group which you till take in its entirety. You will have fifty-five coins in total, and when you place them on the scale it would read 55 ounces if all of the coins were real. Because you have taken a sample from each group you know that the scale will read less than that. If the scale reads 54.5 ounces you know that there is one counterfeit coin in the group, so you know that the group of counterfeits is the first group which you took a sample of only one coin from. If the scale reads 54 ounces you know there are two counterfeit coins on the scale, so it must be group two. This way of weighing will lead you directly to the stack of counterfeits. Elegant.

28. Two Hourglasses

SOLUTION

This is a personal favorite. This riddle is outstanding because it is very easy to remember, very easy to tell, very easy to solve without pen and paper, and very elegant.

The solution: Flip both timers. When the seven-minute timer runs out, turn the eleven-minute timer on its side. There are four minutes remaining in the eleven-minute timer. Now flip the seven-minute timer and start it again at the same time you turn the eleven-minute timer back up, running the four minutes out of it. Once the eleven-minute timer is empty, turn the seven-minute timer sideways. You now have four-minutes of sand in the seven-minute timer. Now all you need to do is start the eleven-minute timer and as soon as it is empty you flip the seven-minute timer and run the four additional minutes out, bringing you to fifteen minutes.

29. <u>Last Words?</u>

SOLUTION

Assuming you'd like to live, the best thing you could tell your executioner is: "Tomorrow morning you will behead me!" If they behead him the statement is true, and if they hang him his statement will have been false.

Your cleverness may be rewarded and your life may be spared.

30. <u>An Evil Mayor</u>

SOLUTION

All the daughter needs to do is remove one stone from the bag and keep it concealed in her hand, and ask the mayor to show the remaining stone to the village. The village will then believe that the farmer's daughter has drawn the white stone.

31. <u>Mixing Medicine</u>

SOLUTION

The key to this riddle is to break the pills in half. Take all three pills from the floor and break them each in half. Split the halves up equally into two piles so that both piles contain one half of each of the three pills. Now you take one pill of Medicine X out of the bottle and split it in half and put one half in each pile. Now you have two piles that each contain two halves of Medicine X and two halves of Medicine Y, which is your appropriate daily dosage.

32. Three Light Bulbs & Three Switches

SOLUTION

In order to determine which switches go with which light bulbs, this is what you must do:

- ◆ Turn the first light switch on.

- ◆ Turn the second light switch on.

- ◆ Leave the third light switch off.

- ◆ Wait 15 minutes and turn the second light switch off.

Now, enter the room with the light bulbs. One light bulb will be on and controlled by the first switch, because it's the only switch that's currently turned on. Of the two light bulbs remaining, both of which are off, one will be hot to the touch because it had just been left on for 15 minutes. The second switch controls this light bulb and the final switch which had remained off the whole time controls the light bulb that is off and not hot.

33. A Spinning Disk

SOLUTION

You would need no more than two sensors to determine which direction the disk is spinning. Placing the sensors right next to each other and simply looking at which lights up first will show you the correct direction.

34. <u>Bridge Crossing</u>

SOLUTION

Alan, Bob, Cal, and Dan can all cross the bridge safely in no less than seventeen minutes. First, Alan and Bob cross the bridge together in two minutes. Alan then comes back with the flashlight in one minute. Cal and Dan then cross the bridge together in ten minutes. Bob returns with the flashlight in two minutes. Finally, Alan and Bob cross the bridge once again in two minutes, which results in everyone being on the other side of the bridge in a total of seventeen minutes.

35. <u>Force Field Detainment</u>

SOLUTION

It should suffice to make the following threat: "I will shoot the first prisoner that steps outside of the force field!"

36. <u>Mexican Laser Standoff</u>

SOLUTION

To maximize your chance of survival you should shoot your laser at the ground in front of you. The turn would then pass to the cyborg with 50% accuracy who would aim at the 100% accurate cyborg, for if he shoots at you and kills you, the 100% cyborg would be up next to shoot and would surely kill him. If the 50% cyborg hits his target and kills the 100% cyborg, it is once again your turn and you have a 25% chance to kill the 50% cyborg and win the duel. If the 50% cyborg misses the 100% cyborg, it will then be the 100% cyborg's turn to shoot, and he will surely aim at the 50% cyborg because he would rather eliminate him from the game than you because you have a worse chance to hit. Once this happens, it will again be your shot and you have a 25% chance to kill the 100% cyborg and win the duel. Thus, hitting the ground is your best option.

Had you aimed at either of the two cyborgs for your first shot and killed them, it would be the remaining cyborg's turn and they would have no other target to aim for but you, and they are both much better shots so you are much more likely to survive if you are able to shoot first. Shooting at the ground guarantees this.

37. A Duck In The Pond

SOLUTION

Although this riddle requires an elementary knowledge of geometry, I felt that it needed to be included because it is also solvable by intuition alone without knowing the formulas and displays an elegance unique to math.

Assume that the radius of the circle is 1 meter, that the duck swims at 1 meter per second, and that the wolf runs at an amazingly fast 4 meters per second. Assume also that the duck has an understanding of geometry and is smarter than most humans that you know. The duck must position itself in the center of the pond. Once centered, the duck can swim to any point that is closer than 0.25 meters from the center and start swimming in a sub-circle that he can swim around faster than the wolf can run around the pond because the circumference of this sub-circle is less than ¼ the circumference of the pond. This means that the duck can position himself at the opposite side of the sub-circle from the wolf. Once opposite the wolf, the duck only needs to swim 0.75 meters to reach the edge of the pond, while the wolf has to run a distance of pi (3.14 meters) to get to that point. This will take the duck 0.75 seconds to do, and will take the wolf 0.785 seconds to do. This gives the duck a whole 0.035 seconds to start flying before the wolf can get to him.

If that amount of time feels too unreasonable to satisfy you as an answer, remember that you can define the pond to be any size you'd like. The larger the pond, the more of a time difference there will be between the time the duck reaches the edge of the pond and the time the wolf gets there.

Alternatively, keeping the pond the same size and slowing down the duck and wolf considerably will provide the same effect.

38. <u>Racehorses</u>

SOLUTION

You can determine your three fastest horses in seven races:

The first thing you have to do is split all of the horses into five groups of five and race them. You must keep track of the positions that each horse comes in. An easy way to do this is to label the races "A", "B", "C", "D", and "E". Then you can label each horse according to the position they came in in the races. For example, the winning horse of race A would be labeled "A1" and the second place finisher would be "A2", and so on and so forth. For the sixth race, you will race the top finishers of the original five races against each other (A1, B1, C1, D1, and E1). The winner of this race is your fastest horse.

As an example, let's assume that the sixth race finished in the following order: D1, B1, A1, C1, E1. You know that C1 and E1 cannot be in the top three among all horses because they lost to D1, B1, and A1. You also know that C2-C5 and E2-E5 cannot be in the top three because they were all slower than C1 and E1. You also know that A2-A5 cannot be in the top three because they are slower than A1, B1, and D1. You also know that B3-B5 cannot be in the top three because they are slower than B2, B1, and D1. This leaves you only five possible horses that can contend for the second-fastest and third-fastest position: D2, D3, B1, B2, and A1.

Race these five horses against each other and the first and second place finishers are your second-fastest and third-fastest horses, respectively.

39. A Dozen Weighted Balls

SOLUTION

You can find the odd ball and whether it is heavier or lighter in only three weighings. To start, you should separate the balls into three groups of four. For the first weighing, put a group of four on either side of the scale. Three things can happen: If the pans balance, you know that those eight balls are all regular and that the odd ball is one of the four balls of unknown weight that you didn't put on the scale. If the left side of the pan goes down, then you know one of the balls in the left pan is heavier than the others or that one of the balls in the right pan is lighter than the others. If the left side of the pan goes up, the opposite is true. Consider these groups of balls "potentially heavier" and "potentially lighter".

If the pans balanced on the first weighing: You now must take three of the four balls of unknown weight and three balls of regular weight and weigh them against each other. If the pans balance this time you know that the odd ball is the ball of unknown weight that you did not put on the scale and you must then take that ball and weigh it against a ball that is known to be of regular weight. This will tell you if the odd ball is heavier or lighter and you will have found it and its weight in only three weighings.

If the pans did not balance on the first weighing: You now must take two "potentially heavier" balls and one "potentially lighter" ball and weigh these three against one "potentially heavier", one "potentially lighter", and one ball of regular weight.

◆ If the pans balance, you now know that all of the balls on the scale are of regular weight and the odd ball must be one of the three balls that are not on the scale. If this is the case you must take the two "potentially lighter" balls that you didn't yet put on the scale and weigh them against each other. If the pans balance this time you know the odd ball out is the "potentially heavier" and you now know that it is indeed heavier. If the pans do not balance, you will easily know which of the two "potentially lighter" balls is the odd and lighter ball.

(solution continued on next page)

◆ If the pans do not balance and the left side of the scale (containing two "potentially heavier" balls and one "potentially lighter" ball) goes down, then you know that the odd ball is either one of these two "potentially heavier" balls or the "potentially lighter" ball that is on the other side of the scale. Now you would take these two "potentially heavier" balls and weigh them against each other. If the pans balance this time, you know that the odd ball is that "potentially lighter" ball from the right side of the scale, and it is indeed lighter. If the pans do not balance, you will easily know which of the two "potentially heavier" balls is the odd and heavier ball.

◆ If the pans do not balance and the right side of the scale (containing one "potentially heavier" ball, one "potentially lighter" ball, and one ball of regular weight) goes down, then you know that the odd ball is either the "potentially heavier" ball on the right side of the scale or the "potentially lighter" ball on the left side of the scale. You must now take this "potentially heavier" ball and weigh it against a ball that is known to be of regular weight. If the pans balance, then the odd ball is the "potentially lighter" ball from the left side of the scale and the ball is indeed lighter. If the pans do not balance, then the "potentially heavier" ball is obviously heavier than the ball of regular weight and is quite odd itself.

40. <u>Two Cups And A Bucket</u>

SOLUTION

If you were to place the two cups into a freezer and freeze the water inside of them, you could easily distinguish the cups of water from one another once they're put into the bucket.

41. <u>Don't Marry That One!</u>

SOLUTION

Let us refer to the three sisters as the truth-teller (T), the liar (L), and the random answerer (R). The key to this solution is understanding that there are six possible configurations that the sisters can be standing in:

TLR - TRL - LTR - LRT - RTL - RLT

Approach the first sister and ask her, "If I were to ask one of your two sisters if the sister standing in the middle of you three sometimes lies and sometimes tells the truth, could they say yes?"

<u>If you get a "yes" answer</u>: This does not tell you anything about the first sister, but it does tell you that the sisters are standing in one of the following orders: RTL, RLT, TLR, or LTR. This shows you that it would be safe to marry the sister standing in the middle.

<u>If you get a "no" answer</u>: then the sisters are standing in one of the following orders: RTL, RLT, TRL, or LRT. This shows you that it would be safe to marry the sister standing last in line. So no matter what the answer to your initial question is, you can safely pick one of the girls to marry.

42. <u>King Arthur's Coin Game</u>

SOLUTION

This strategy guarantees success for the first player of the game:

For your first move, place a coin directly in the middle of the table. After each coin your opponent places you just need to place your coin in the opposite spot.

By first placing a coin in the middle of the table and then mirroring your opponent, you will always have a place for your coins and your opponent will run out of room first.

43. The Bronx vs. Brooklyn

SOLUTION

This situation is happening simply because the train to Brooklyn arrives one minute after the train to The Bronx.

44. Three Playing Cards

SOLUTION

The three cards are the King of Hearts, the Jack of Hearts, and the King of Clubs, in that order.

45. Colored Weights

SOLUTION

To find the heavier weight of each color you only need to use the balance scale twice. First, you must weigh a red and a white weight against a blue and a white weight.

If the pans balance: You can be sure that there is a heavy and a light weight on each pan. Take both the red and blue weights off the scale and leave the white weights on each side. This will show you which of the white weights is the heavier one, which will then show you whether the red or blue weight that was just on the pan was the heavier one, which will then allow you to by process of elimination determine the weight of the red and blue weight that were never on the pan.

If the pans do not balance: You can be sure that the white weight on the side of the scale that went down is the heavier of the two white weights. To find the heavier weight of the red and blue pair, you must take the red weight that you just weighed and weigh it against the blue weight that has not yet been on the scale. Seeing what happens here plus remembering what happened when you made the first weighing will allow you to correctly label each weight.

46. Calendar Cubes

SOLUTION

The key to the solution is the fact that "6" and "9" are the same character. One cube would contain the numbers 0, 1, 2, 3, 4, and 5. The other cube would contain the numbers 0, 1, 2, 6, 7, and 8. Even though there is no day "00" a zero is needed on both cubes in order to make all of the days between "01" and "09". There are many alternate configurations that also will produce all of the days of the month.

47. <u>Finding Your Seat</u>

SOLUTION

Believe it or not, the probability of your seat being available when you board the plane is 1/2. This problem may be easier to understand if you start by reducing the number of passengers in line to two. Now think about the problem with three passengers, four passengers, and then five passengers. You will quickly see that the chance of you getting your own seat is going to be 50% no matter how many people are involved.

Here's another way to think about the problem: If any of the first forty-nine passengers sit in your seat, you will not get to sit in your seat. But, if any of the first forty-nine passengers sit in the first passenger's seat, you will definitely get to sit in your seat. It will always be equally likely that a passenger in line sits in either the first passenger's seat or your seat if they are unable to sit in their own seat.

48. Three Prospective Employees

SOLUTION

Alan knows that he is wearing a black hat and this is how he is able to deduce it: It is clear, because all three men raised their hands, that there are at least two black hats. However, if there were two black hats and one white hat, either of the men with the black hats would see the white hat and see that everyone had their hand raised which would allow him to instantly deduce the color of their hat.

After a few seconds had passed without anyone speaking about the color of their hat, it became clear to Alan, the brightest of the bunch, that they must all be wearing black hats or else either Bob or Cal, who are perfectly intelligent, would have said something by now.

49. <u>Late To Work</u>

SOLUTION

Alan is wearing a black hat and he deduced this quite easily. Each man is instructed to raise their hand if they see at least two black hats. All four men raised their hand, which means that there were either three or four black hats.

If there were only two black hats then only the two men with white hats would raise their hands, for each man in a black hat would only see one other. However, if all four men had black hats on, no one would be able to deduce anything and Alan wouldn't have been able to come to a conclusion.

Alan is wearing a black hat and sees two black hats and a white hat. He was able to deduce that his hat was black because if each of the men with black hats raised their hands, then that means they each saw two black hats and because Alan sees one white hat, he knows that he must be the 'other' black hat for each of those two men.

50. Intellectuals Standing In Line With Hats

SOLUTION

For this solution lets start at the back of the line with Alan, who can see all three hats in front of him. Because there needs to be one hat of each color on the men's heads, Alan is able to deduce the color of his hat only if he sees just two different colors ahead of him. Assume he sees two red hats and a blue hat:

Alan can be positive that his hat is white, which is his correct answer.

Bob, who can see two hats in front of him and knows that Alan is correct, knows that he cannot be wearing a white hat or else Alan would have answered differently. If he sees a hat of each remaining color, red and blue, in front of him, he would not be sure which color hat he is wearing and therefore Bob must see two of the same color hats in front of him. We will assume Bob sees two red hats, allowing him to deduce that his hat is blue, which is his correct answer.

Cal, trusting that Alan and Bob both gave the correct answer, would know that his hat had to be the same color as the one in front of him or else Bob wouldn't have been able to deduce the color of his own hat. Cal, seeing a red hat in front of him, deduces that his hat must be red as well, which is his correct answer.

Dan, the final person in line who can see no hats, is able to understand the situation the same way it was just explained in this solution, and has a quite simple answer. He knows that Alan must have seen only two colors and he heard Alan's answer of white. He knows that Bob must have seen two of the same color in front of him or else he wouldn't have been able to correctly give his answer of blue. Knowing these things, Dan only needs to give the same answer as Cal, for the two of them must be wearing the same color hat.

51. <u>Numbered Foreheads</u>

SOLUTION

When Claude asks you for the second time if you know what your number is you confidently reply, "Well yes I do, and my number is 50!"

When you first look at Eugene and Frank and see the numbers 20 and 30, you can deduce that your number has to be either 10 or 50 because one number has to be the sum of the other two. Knowing that Eugene and Frank both said "no" allows you to deduce that your number must be 50.

This is true because if your number was 10, Frank would have seen the number 20 on Eugene's head and the number 10 on your head and known that his number must be 30 because the only options for his number in that situation are 10 and 30, and his number could not have been 10 because there can only be one of each number.

52. <u>Rope Burning</u>

SOLUTION

The key to this solution lies in what happens when you light the ropes from both ends. If the ropes take one hour to burn completely, then when you light a rope from both ends it will take half the time because the consumption rate of the fire is doubled.

To time forty-five minutes, you must do this: Light the first rope from both ends and the second rope from just one end. Once the first rope is completely burnt, you will know that thirty minutes have gone by and you will know that the second rope has thirty minutes of time left before it burns completely. As soon as the first rope is completely burnt you light the other end of the second rope, which will double the rate of consumption and cut the remaining time in the rope in half, meaning that it will only take fifteen more minutes for the second rope to burn out completely.

The thirty minutes from the first rope and the fifteen minutes from the second rope gives you forty-five minutes.

53. <u>A Stopped Watch</u>

SOLUTION

All the old man did was set his watch to run backwards.

54. Hotel Security

SOLUTION

Securely sending the valuable ring is actually quite simple. First, Alan must put the ring in the safe and lock the safe with his lock. He keeps his key and sends the safe over to Bob through the bellhops. The box is locked and safe. Bob then receives the safe and attaches his lock to it, keeping his key and sending the safe back to Alan, this time with two locks attached. Alan then unlocks his lock and removes it from the safe and sends it back over to Bob, who simply unlocks his lock with his key and opens the safe.

55. The Secret of Monk Island

SOLUTION

At midnight there are many things that can happen on the island depending on how many blue-eyed monks there are:

If there is only one monk with blue eyes he will commit suicide that night. After hearing the man say that at least one of the monks has blue eyes the monks all look at each other. If there was only one monk with blue eyes he would look around at everyone else and see only brown-eyed monks which would unfortunately for him tell him that he himself has the blue eyes.

If there were two monks with blue eyes, each one would see one monk with blue eyes and on the first night neither would commit suicide, hoping that the blue-eyed monk that they saw was the only one with blue eyes. After the first night each of the two blue-eyed monks would see the other still alive and know that they must also have blue eyes themselves, for if they didn't then the other blue-eyed monk would have seen only brown-eyes monks and would have known that they had blue eyes and committed suicide. The second night, both of the blue-eyed monks would know that they have blue eyes and would kill themselves.

This line of reasoning continues forever and works for any number of blue-eyed monks. If one monk has blue eyes, he will know on the first day and kill himself on the first night. If two monks have blue eyes, they will know on the second day and kill themselves on the second night. If three monks have blue eyes, they will know on the third day and kill themselves on the third night. So on and so forth until there are no more suicides and the monks can go on living in peace, knowing that they all have beautiful brown eyes.

56. Flipping Quarters

SOLUTION

You can win this game with just one elegant move: Take any twenty coins from the hundred, put them into a separate pile, and flip them over.

No matter how many of the coins are tails in the group you flip over, you will always wind up with two groups of coins with the same number of tails. If you happened to select all twenty of the coins that were already tails, you would separate them and flip them, resulting in two groups of coins with zero tails in them. If you happened to select twenty coins with only six tails among them you would leave fourteen tails in the original pile and after flipping the twenty coins you selected you would have fourteen tails and six heads in the new pile. This will always work as long as you only take twenty coins, put them into their own pile, and flip them all over.

57. <u>Truth, Falsehood, Randomness</u>

SOLUTION

This is a very difficult riddle. The key is realizing the importance of first asking a question regarding the positions of each man in relation to one another. To begin, we will look at the six possible states for the order of the truth-teller (T), the liar (L), and the random-answerer (R) standing next to one another:

TRL - TLR - LRT - LTR - RTL - RLT

To begin, ask the person first in line if the liar is standing to the left (from our point of view) of the random-answerer:

♦ If the answer is a "yes" then you know it has to be either the truth-teller telling you the truth, the liar lying, or a random answer from the random-answerer. This leaves four possible situations regarding who the men are:

TLR - LTR - RTL - RLT

♦ If the answer is a "no" then it again has to be either the truth-teller telling you the truth, the liar lying, or a random answer from the random-answerer. This too leaves four possible situations regarding who the men are:

TRL - LRT - RTL - RLT

Now, based on the answer to the first question, you can be sure that your next questions are directed to the truth-teller or the liar and you can avoid speaking to the random-answerer.

(solution continued on next page)

The second question will isolate the liar and the truth-teller. Based on the answer to the first question you asked you will ask one of the men: "Is the truth-teller standing in line?"

- If the answer to the first question was a "yes" then you will ask this question to the second person in line, who is definitely not the random-answerer.

- If the answer to the first question was a "no" then you will ask this question to the third person in line, who is definitely not the random-answerer.

The answer to the second question will give even more information about the position of the men. You know that if the answer to your second question is a "yes" that you have asked the truth-teller and if the answer to your second question is a "no" then you have asked the liar.

Knowing this and the answer to the first question, you can reduce the possibilities of who is who down to these four situations:

- If both answers were "yes" it has to be LTR or RTL.

- If both answers were "no" it has to be TRL or RTL.

- If the first answer was "yes" and the second answer was "no" it has to be TLR or RLT.

- If the first answer was "no" and the second answer was "yes" it has to be LRT or RLT.

The final question is simple. Because you can be sure of the position of either the truth-teller or the liar after the second question and because you know that each man knows the identity of each other man, asking them a question about one of the remaining two men will reveal the identity of both of them and give you the solution. For example, if the answers to the first two questions were both "yes", you know that the two possible configurations are LTR or RTL. Between the two of these, you can be sure that if you ask the second person in line a question, he will answer truthfully because either way it is the truth-teller. In this case, you could ask him: "Is the first person in line the liar?" His answer will tell you who the first person in line is and by the simplest process of elimination you then are sure of the last person in line as well.

58. <u>The Stolen Blue Carbuncle</u>

SOLUTION

The three thieves have quite a system set up. The system reveals enough information to the thieves so that they are sure as to whether or not one of them stole the blue carbuncle, but not enough information to tell any one thief who did it. Additionally, the system does not allow for the surveillance team to even know whether or not *any* of the men at the table were involved with the theft.

Each thief sees only two flips of the coin, both flips being the same or each flip being different, and each thief either stole the blue carbuncle or they did not steal it. This presents four possible scenarios for each thief, each of which is associated with the winking of an eye:

    ◆   If they stole the gem and both flips were the same, they will wink their right eye.

    ◆   If they did not steal the gem and both flips were the same, they will wink their left eye.

    ◆   If they stole the gem and both flips were different, they will wink their left eye.

    ◆   If they did not steal the gem and both flips were different, they will wink their right eye.

Based on the winks, the information is communicated perfectly:

    ◆   If none of the thieves stole the blue carbuncle, there will be either three right winks or two left winks and one right wink.

    ◆   If one of the thieves stole the blue carbuncle, there will be either three left winks or two right winks and a left wink.

Because the surveillance team can only see two of the winks, they can never be sure what has happened, even if they learn the system that the thieves are using.

59. <u>Three Locks</u>

SOLUTION

The system to allow for any two thieves to access the contents of the safe but disallow any one thief alone from entering is actually quite simple:

First, each thief picks which buttons they are going to push. Then, each thief in turn pushes the buttons however they decided to push them. After each thief has pushed the buttons, thief one tells thief two which buttons he pushed, thief two tells thief three which buttons he pushed, and thief three tells thief one which buttons he pushed.

By doing this, any group of two thieves will know all three thieves actions and can apply them again in turn which will return the locks to their initial state, completely deactivated. However, any one thief will not have enough information to return the locks to their initial states because they will only know two of the three sets of actions.

60. <u>Bear Hunting</u>

SOLUTION

The bear that tore up the hunter's cabin must have been a white polar bear. The only way for this hunter to have travelled the way he travelled and wind up back at his starting point would be if he were at the North Pole.

61. <u>Blind Man's Socks</u>

SOLUTION

These intelligent blind men realized that if each pair of socks was rubber banded together they could collect six pairs each and split the contents of each pair with one another. This assures them that no matter what color socks they picked up, they would both wind up with six socks of one color and six socks of the other color.

For example, if the first man picked up all six pairs of black socks and the second man picked up all six pairs of the white socks they could split each pair between the two of them and they would wind up with six white socks and six black socks each, giving them their initial three pairs of whites and three pairs of blacks.

62. <u>Five Greedy Pirates</u>

SOLUTION

The solution to this riddle is easily reached if you work backwards.

Assume that only Pirate E is alive and all four others have been thrown overboard. There is only one possible scenario here: Pirate E will take all one hundred pieces of the gold uncontested and there will be no one to throw him overboard.

Now look at the situation if Pirate D and Pirate E are the only ones alive: Because there is only one vote needed when there are two pirates, Pirate D will take all one hundred gold coins uncontested.

If Pirate C, Pirate D, and Pirate E are alive: Pirate C needs to win one vote in addition to his own, which will be easy and most affordable to do if he gives Pirate E just one piece of gold and keeps the rest for himself. Pirate E will vote for this allocation because his alternative is the situation described above. Pirate D will never vote for Pirate C's allocation unless he gets all one hundred gold coins because if Pirate C's suggestion does not pass, Pirate D will be guaranteed to wind up with all of the gold.

If Pirate B, Pirate C, Pirate D, and Pirate E are alive: Pirate B also only needs to win one vote in addition to his own. One way he can do this is to give Pirate E two coins and keep the rest for himself. Pirate E will vote for this allocation because it is better than his alternative, which is described above. A smarter thing for Pirate B to do is to give Pirate D just one coin and keep the other ninety-nine for himself. Pirate D will vote for this allocation because his alternative is the situation above, a situation where he ends up with zero gold coins.

Finally, if all five pirates are alive and involved in the voting and Pirate A has to come up with an allocation: Pirate A will propose keeping ninety-eight coins for himself, giving one coin to Pirate C, and giving one coin to Pirate E. Because there are five voting participants, there needs to be three votes for the allocation. Pirate A can ensure his allocation is supported by the majority if he keeps ninety-eight coins for himself and gives one coin to Pirate C and one coin to either Pirate E or Pirate D. Pirate C and either Pirate E or Pirate D will vote for this because their alternative is the situation above, which could leave them both with nothing.

63. <u>Stealing Bell Ropes</u>

SOLUTION

You can acquire all two hundred feed of the rope and wind up safely on the ground. First, tie the bottoms of the ropes together to make one long rope. Then, climb up one rope all the way to the ceiling and untie the other rope from the hook. With the end of this newly untied rope in your hand, fish it through both hooks and lower it down to the ground. Then you can untie the other end of the rope and while holding onto both of them lower yourself safely to the ground. Then pull on one side of the rope until it fishes itself back through the hooks and falls to the ground.

64. <u>Three Coins</u>

SOLUTION

The fewest number of steps you need to take in order to guarantee winning your friend's game is three.

No matter what the initial state is, following these three steps will guarantee that you win:

- ◆ Flip any two of the three coins.

- ◆ Flip any one of the two coins that you just flipped.

- ◆ Flip both of those coins again.

65. Two Trees And An Island

SOLUTION

First, tie one end of the rope to the tree next to you. Then, while you are holding the other end of the rope, walk all the way around the lake. This will wrap the rope around the tree in the center. When you return to your starting point, tie the end of the rope you are holding to the large tree. You can now use this makeshift rope bridge to hold on to and cross the lake to the island.

66. <u>A Camel & Bananas</u>

SOLUTION

The maximum amount of bananas you can take to the town with your camel is five hundred and thirty-three. This is achieved by a trip consisting of optimized segments:

First, load the camel up with 1000 bananas and travel 200 miles. At the 200-mile mark, leave 600 of the 800 uneaten bananas there and travel 200 miles back to the starting point. All 800 bananas cannot be left at the 200-mile mark because the camel needs to be fed in order to make the trip back to the starting point. Do this twice more, but on the third trip stay at the 200-mile point.

Now you are at the 200-mile point with 2000 bananas. Load the camel up with 1000 bananas again, move 333 miles to the 533-mile point, leave 334 of the 667 uneaten bananas there, and travel back to the 200-mile point.

Load the camel up with the remaining 1000 bananas and travel 333 miles to the 533-mile point again, adding 667 uneaten bananas to the total.

Now you are at the 533-mile point with 1001 bananas. Load the camel up with 1000 bananas, eat the extra one, and travel the remaining 467 miles to arrive in town with 533 uneaten bananas.

67. Trapped In A Room

SOLUTION

You can escape from the room in seven steps or less. When solving this riddle it is important to think about the four possible states for the room to be in initially:

- ◆ State A: One button is "on" and three buttons are "off".

- ◆ State B: Two buttons are "on" and on opposing walls.

- ◆ State C: Two buttons are "on" and on adjacent walls.

- ◆ State D: Three buttons are "on" and one button is "off".

Initially, you cannot be sure which of these four states the room is in.

Your first move is to push two buttons on opposing walls. If the room was in State B you will be freed. If the room was in State C it will stay in State C. If the room was in either State A or State D it will remain in either State A or State D.

Next, if you were not freed, push two buttons on adjacent walls. If the room was in State C you will either be freed or the room will turn into State B. If the room was in either State A or State D it will again remain in either State A or State D.

Then, if you were not freed, push two buttons on opposing walls again. If the room was in State B you will be freed. If the room was in State A or State D it will still remain in either State A or State D. If you are still not free at this point, you can be sure that the room is in either State A or State D. Now, press any one button and you will be certain that you are in a room that is either in State B or State C.

Finally, repeat the steps from the beginning. Because the room is either in State B or State C, you will be free in a maximum of three more steps.

68. Past, Present, & Future

SOLUTION

The first part of this riddle that needs to be solved is the "da" and "ya" situation. Even without knowing what "da" and "ya" mean there is a way you can phrase each question and be sure of what the gods' answers are.

For example, if you ask a god: "Does 'da' mean 'yes' if and only if your favorite color is red?" you can be sure that the god's favorite color is red if he answers with a 'da' and you can be sure that the god's favorite color is not red if he answers with a "ya". This is the structure with which all three questions need to be asked to the gods. You also need to think of the three gods as "God 1", "God 2", and "God 3".

There are many different sets of questions that you can ask in order to determine which god is which. The following is one elegant solution:

- The first question is directed to God 1: "Is God 2 Future?"

- The second question is directed to God 1 again: "Is God 2 Present?"

- The third question is directed to God 3 if the answer to the second question was yes and directed to God 1 if the answer to the second question was no: "Is God 1 Future?"

Keep in mind that these three questions need to be asked in the structure that allows you to disregard the language barrier.

69. <u>Figuring Out Numbers</u>

SOLUTION

This is an absolutely amazing riddle. At first glance it seems as if there is not enough information to come up with the solution, but if the situation is broken down into the proper pieces there is a clarity that develops that will lead you to the single answer if you can follow it. Remember, Alan and Bob are perfectly intelligent mathematicians.

The solution starts with Alan, who knows the product of the two numbers. Because Alan says he cannot tell what the two numbers are, it is known that the product can be produced by multiple sets of numbers. For example, if Alan knew that the product was 50 he wouldn't know if the two numbers were 5 and 10 or 2 and 25. This tells you that the two numbers cannot both be prime numbers (a number that cannot be evenly divided by anything other than itself and 1) or else they would be the only set of numbers that produced their product (since one of the numbers cannot be 1) and Alan would know what they were.

Bob's response, "I already knew you couldn't" adds important new information. If Bob already knew that Alan couldn't have possibly known the two numbers then it can be deduced that the sum that Bob knows cannot be any number that can be made by adding together two prime numbers. This means that the sum of the two numbers cannot be even and it cannot be two more than a prime number. This reduces the list of numbers that can be Bob's sum to: 11, 17, 23, 27, 29, 35, 37, 41, 47, 51, 53, 57, 59, 63, 65, 67, 71, 77, 79, 83, 87, 89, 93, 95, or 99.

Alan's next statement is very interesting: "Ah, now I know the numbers!"

At this point, Alan knows the product of the two numbers and now all of the possible sums of the two numbers, which allows him to positively figure out the two numbers themselves. This means that out of all of the factors of the two numbers' product there must be multiple sets that add up to multiple different sums, but one and only one set of factors that add up to a number on Bob's list of possible sums.

(*solution continued on next page*)

Bob then replies with: "Now I know them too!"

At this point in the conversation Bob knows the sum of the two numbers and the ten sums that were listed above (if we can figure these numbers out ourselves then Bob must be able to as well because we both have the same information). Bob also knows that Alan knows not only the product of the two numbers but now the two numbers themselves. After thinking about all of these things, Bob is also able to deduce the two numbers.

There is no trick here; Bob also knows that Alan's product must have multiple factors but only one set that adds up to one of the numbers in the list of sums. At that point, it is just 'trial and error' by Bob to finally find that the two numbers must be 4 and 13, the product is 52, and the sum is 17. This is the unique solution and satisfies each statement in the short conversation.

70. The Switchers

SOLUTION

To determine which man is the truth-teller you must ask two questions. First, you ask any one of the five men in front of you, "Are you the truth-teller?" The answer will either be "yes" or "no".

If the answer was "yes" then the person you asked is either the truth-teller telling the truth, or a Switcher lying. You also know that if you ask that same person a question again, they have to tell you the truth, because the person is either the truth-teller, who always tells the truth, or a lying Switcher, who would then have to tell you the truth since he just lied to you. In this situation, your second question will be to the same person and it will be: "Who is the truth-teller?" If the first person you asked was the truth-teller then he will answer your second question by saying: "I am the truth-teller!" and if the first person you asked was a lying Switcher, he will answer your question by telling you which of the remaining four people is the truth-teller.

If the answer to the first question was "no" then the person you asked must be a Switcher telling the truth. This means that if you ask this person a question again they will be forced to lie to you. So ask the same person the following question: "Who is not the truth-teller?" Because they have to lie to you, the only way for them to answer that question is to identify the truth-teller, for if they told you that another one of the Switchers was the truth-teller they would be answering your question truthfully.

71. <u>Making Ice</u>

SOLUTION

The maximum amount of full-sized ice cubes you can make in sixty minutes is two hundred and twenty-eight.

To make this many ice cubes you must stack the seven trays as follows: Fill one tray up with water and put it in the bottom of the freezer. Then, take an empty tray, flip it over, and place it on top of the first tray. Now you can place another full tray of water on top of this empty tray. This technique enables you to make four full trays of ice cubes in the first fifteen minutes without any trays sinking into each other. After you have made the first forty-eight ice cubes, empty all of the trays. Now, place one ice cube into each of the four corners of six of the trays. You can now fill the remaining eight slots in each of these trays with water and safely stack them on top of each other in the freezer. The seventh tray does not need to be stacked on top of so this can be filled completely with water. This will produce an additional sixty ice cubes in the next fifteen minutes. Repeat this twice more to produce a total of two hundred and twenty-eight ice cubes in just one hour.

72. The Blue Forehead Room

SOLUTION

What happens in this situation, since the hundred people are all perfectly intelligent logicians, seems odd if you only know what happens and do not know why it happens: The lights turn on for the first time and each logician looks around and sees ninety-nine blue foreheads. Then the lights get turned off for a few minutes and turned back on. When the lights are turned on the second time, each logician looks around and still sees ninety-nine blue foreheads. No one has left the room. This continues on and on until the lights get turned on for the hundredth time. After the lights are turned on for the hundredth time, all one hundred logicians are still standing in the room. Finally, the lights get turned off and all one hundred of the logicians exit the room at the same time.

Reducing the number of people in the room helps to display the reason why everyone exits together on the hundredth flip of the switch.

Think about what happens if there is only one person in the room: He would enter for the first time, the lights would turn on, and when the lights turn off he would exit the room because he knows that at least one person has to have a blue forehead and he is the only person in the room.

Now think about what happens if there are two people in the room: They would enter for the first time (both with blue foreheads), the lights would turn on, and they would see the other person's blue forehead. The lights will turn off and neither man will exit the room because neither of them knows anything about the color of their own forehead. The lights turn on for the second time and the men realize that they both must have blue foreheads, for if one of them did not have a blue forehead the other man would have seen his non-blue forehead and been able to deduce that he must have a blue forehead himself since one of them has to, causing him to exit the room the first night. So, when the lights get turned off for the second time, both men will exit the room at the same time.

(solution continued on next page)

Now think about what happens if there are three people in the room but only two of them have blue foreheads: They would all enter the room and the lights would be turned on for the first time. Two of the logicians with blue foreheads will see one other man with a blue forehead and one man without a blue forehead. The logician that does not have a blue forehead will see two other men with blue foreheads. Each of the logicians with blue foreheads will exit the room after the light has been turned on two times because they have each deduced the following: "If I do not have a blue forehead, the man I see with a blue forehead will know that he himself has a blue forehead and leave the room the first time the lights are turned off. But, if I have a blue forehead the man I see with a blue forehead will not leave the room the first time the lights are turned off. When the lights get turned on the second time and we both see each other again, we will know that we must both have blue foreheads for if only one of us had a blue forehead they would have been able to deduce that the first time the lights were turned on and would have left the room."

If all three logicians in the room had their foreheads painted blue the line of reasoning above would extend for one more day and all three men would be able to deduce that they must all have blue foreheads and exit together when the lights are turned off. Each additional man with a blue forehead you add to the group will result in one more required switch of the lights before all men exit. This is why the lights will turn on one hundred times without anything happening and then as soon as the lights turn off for the hundredth time everyone will leave together.

73. The Game Show

SOLUTION

This is one of the simplest and yet extremely deceptive problems of all time. It is more commonly known as "The Monty Hall Problem" which gets its name from Monty Hall, who was the original host of the American game show "Let's Make A Deal". There is some fun history behind this riddle: Marilyn vos Savant, a woman famous for having a very high IQ (high enough for the Guinness Book of World Records), wrote a column for 'Parade' magazine called 'Ask Marilyn' where readers could write in math-related questions for her to answer. One of the readers sent this riddle in to her and her response caused over ten thousand readers, almost a thousand of which had PhDs, to write to her and tell her she was wrong.

Unfortunately for them, she was right.

Believe it or not, the right move to make in the situation proposed by the riddle is to always switch doors. If you switch doors you will have a 2/3 chance to win the million dollars and if you do not switch doors you will have a 1/3 chance.

An elegant explanation: Assume that you will always choose to switch doors. The only way for you to lose after switching is for you to have initially picked the door with the million dollars behind it. The probability of that happening is definitely and always 1/3, and because of that you will always have a 2/3 probability of winning if you choose to switch doors. Again, if your policy is to always switch doors, then you will always win if you initially picked a door with a goat behind it, and you will always lose if you initially picked the door with the million dollars behind it.

Another explanation: What the game show host is offering you by allowing you to switch doors is effectively the same as the host offering you to select one door and then giving you the opportunity to instead take what is behind both of the doors that you did not pick.

74. <u>One Hundred Prisoners & Two Light Bulbs</u>

SOLUTION

This is a seemingly complex situation with a simple and elegant solution.

It is important to first understand that two light bulbs can only produce four different states:

- ◆ Both bulbs off.

- ◆ Both bulbs on.

- ◆ First bulb off and second bulb on.

- ◆ First bulb on and second bulb off.

This means you can only count to four with two light bulbs. Because you are trying to count to one hundred, there clearly must be another way of doing things. The trick is for the prisoners to designate one person as the "counter", who has a special role, while the other ninety-nine prisoners all obey the following rules:

- ◆ If the prisoner enters the room, has never been in the room before, and both light bulbs are off: He will turn the first light bulb on and exit the room.

- ◆ If the prisoner enters the room, has never been in the room before, and only the first light bulb is on: He will turn the first light bulb off, turn the second light bulb on, and exit the room.

- ◆ If the prisoner enters the room, has never been in the room before, and only the second light bulb is on: He will turn the first light bulb on, so that both bulbs are lit, and exit the room.

- ◆ If the prisoner enters the room, has never been in the room before, and both light bulbs are on: He will do nothing and immediately exit the room.

(solution continued on next page)

- If the prisoner enters the room and has already entered the room once before and changed the states of the light bulbs, he will do nothing and immediately leave the room.

Any time that the counter enters the room, he will observe the state of the light bulbs and do the following:

- If the counter sees only the first light bulb on, he will add one to the count because this means that only one prisoner who has never entered the room before has entered. He will then turn off both bulbs.

- If the counter sees only the second light bulb on, he will add two to the count because this means that only two prisoners who have never entered the room before have entered. He will then turn off both bulbs.

- If the counter sees both light bulbs on, he will add three to the count because this tells him that at least three prisoners who have never entered the room before have entered. He will then turn off both bulbs.

By turning the light bulbs back off after entering the room the counter will 'reset' the bulbs and allow for more prisoners to keep counting. This works because according to the prisoners' plan, once someone has entered the room after already entering the room before and changing the states of the light bulbs, they will do nothing as they have already been accounted for and fulfilled their duty. Once the counter's count reaches ninety-nine he can be sure that all of the prisoners have entered the room at least once and he can tell the warden: "All one hundred of us have been taken to this room since this game has started" and be certain to win the game.

75. A Dozen Hatted Prisoners

SOLUTION

The prisoners can come up with a plan that will give the first prisoner to act a 50/50 chance at survival and will guarantee that the other eleven prisoners in line all survive. This is how they do it:

The prisoners decide that whoever is standing in the twelfth position and speaks first will simply say whichever color they see an even amount of. There is no way for this prisoner to raise his chances of survival above 50% but by saying whichever color he sees an even amount of, every other prisoner can deduce the color of their own hat.

For example:

- If the twelfth person says "black", then the eleventh person in line knows what color hat they are wearing and can correctly state it to the group based on the remaining hats that they can see. If they see an odd number of black hats in front of them then they can be sure that their hat is black because the person in line behind them saw an even amount. Now, the tenth person in line, knowing that the twelfth person saw an even amount of black hats and knowing that the eleventh person in line is wearing a black hat, can deduce the color of their hat based on the remaining nine hats.

- If the twelfth person in line saw an even amount of black hats, and the eleventh person in line is wearing a black hat, then the tenth person in line knows that if he sees an odd number of black hats he is wearing a white hat, and if he sees an even number of black hats he must be wearing a black hat himself.

This system allows for eleven prisoners to guarantee their survival. Not so much fun for the guy in the back of the line.

76. <u>Einstein's Riddle</u>

SOLUTION

The German owns the fish.

This is a very famous riddle. It is often accredited to Albert Einstein despite a lack of any real evidence. The common way to solve this riddle, and any other riddle like it, is to make a table to keep track of all of the known facts.

All of the needed information is in the question. Start with the fact that the Norwegian lives in the first house. It also says that the Norwegian lives next to a blue house, which means that the blue house must be the second house. Next is the fact that the green house is to the left of the white house, which gives you two possible situations. At this point, you should make a new table to account for both possibilities as you continue putting the pieces together. Continuing with the information that you have and slowly putting more facts together will eventually lead you to the answer.

77. The Impossible Rainbow

SOLUTION

If the quality of a riddle were based on the percentage of people who claim it to be impossible, this would likely be the highest-quality riddle of all time. The solution requires the prisoners to follow a very simple yet very deeply complicated system that is grounded in something called modular arithmetic. This is how they do it:

First, the prisoners will number the colors 0 through 6:

- Red = 0
- Green = 3
- Orange = 1
- Blue = 4
- Yellow = 2
- Indigo = 5
- Violet = 6

Then, the prisoners will number themselves 0 through 6 as well. When the game starts the prisoners begin as follows: Each prisoner will add up the number of each of the six hats he sees, and subtract this total from his own personal number.

For example, if Prisoner 4 looked around the circle and saw three orange hats and three blue hats he would add up the value of those six hats, getting a total of 15, and subtract that from his own number, which is 4, and end up with -11.

Then, the prisoners will use modular arithmetic, in the form of "modulo 7", to reduce this number to a number in the range of 0 through 6. To perform a "modulo 7 reduction" on a number you simply add or subtract 7 repeatedly until the number falls into the wanted range. In this case, Prisoner 4 would add 7 to -11 over and over until he ends up with a number between 0 and 6, to do this he will add 7 to -11 twice and arrive at the number 3. The number 3 corresponds to the color green, so Prisoner 4 will guess that he is wearing a green hat. If each of the seven prisoners performs this function and follows these steps, it is guaranteed that at least one of them will guess correctly! A wonderful display of the magic of mathematics.

78. <u>One Hundred Prisoners & One Hundred Boxes</u>

SOLUTION

Believe it or not, the prisoners can adhere to a strategy that will guarantee they are all set free. The strategy that they must use is simple and elegant. Despite its simplicity, the underlying mathematical concepts are quite complex. In the introduction to this book it was said that there should be no riddle that requires complicated mathematics. Some things are worth lying about.

Here's what the prisoners do: First the prisoners will decide the order in which they will enter the room and number each prisoner from 1 to 100, with Prisoner 1 being the first to enter the room and Prisoner 100 being the last. Then, each prisoner must memorize all other prisoner's position in line.

Once the game begins, each prisoner will act in the following manner:

Prisoner 1 will enter the room and open Box 1. If this box does not contain his name, he will go to the box that corresponds with the number associated with the prisoner's name that was in the first box and open it. For example, if the first box contains the name of Prisoner 47, then Prisoner 1 will check Box 47, and if Box 47 contains the name of Prisoner 3, then Prisoner 1 will check Box 3, and so on and so forth. Once Prisoner 1 opens the box that contains his own name, he does not need to continue opening boxes and can exit the room.

Prisoner 2 will then enter the room and start with Box 2, Prisoner 3 will start with Box 3 when he enters, etc.

This strategy by itself will allow for a greater than 30% chance of success, as Prisoner 1 will never have more than a 50% chance of opening the box with his name in it. However, because the warden has allowed for the first prisoner to open all hundred boxes and swap two names if he wants, success can be guaranteed.

(solution continued on next page)

This is because this strategy works on a series of loops. For example: Prisoner 4 opens Box 4 which contains the name of Prisoner 5, then Box 5 which contains the name of Prisoner 37, then Box 37 which contains the name of Prisoner 12, then Box 12 which contains the name of Prisoner 4. This loop goes from Box 4 to Box 5 to Box 37 to Box 12 (which contains Prisoner 4's name).

Every prisoner's name that is opened within this loop will also be guaranteed to find their own name because they each start with the box that corresponds with their number, meaning they will follow through the same loop. When it is Prisoner 37's turn, he will start with Box 37, which takes him to Box 12, and then to Box 4, and then to Box 5, which contains his name. As long as there are no loops inside these boxes that are greater than 50 steps, the prisoners will always win.

An important note: if there is a loop that is over 50 steps long, there can only be one. There cannot be two 51-step loops because that would require 102 boxes. Because the warden has allowed for the first prisoner to open all 100 boxes and swap any two names, the first prisoner can go through each loop and if there does happen to be one that is over 50 steps long he can swap two names from it to cut the loop in half and guarantee the success of the prisoners.

"WHY, SOMETIMES
I'VE BELIEVED AS
MANY AS SIX
IMPOSSIBLE THINGS
BEFORE BREAKFAST."

-Lewis Carroll

57247788R00085

Made in the USA
San Bernardino, CA
19 November 2017